MIRJA WINKELMANN

ONE WORD, TWO MEANINGS

Odd Couples

Can you find the matching word
for each pair of pictures?

Solutions on the last page

Prestel
Munich · London · New York

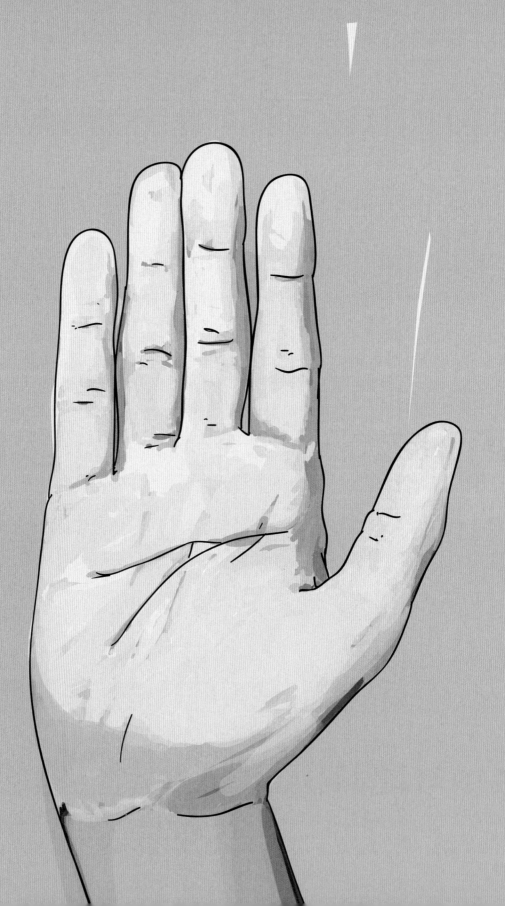

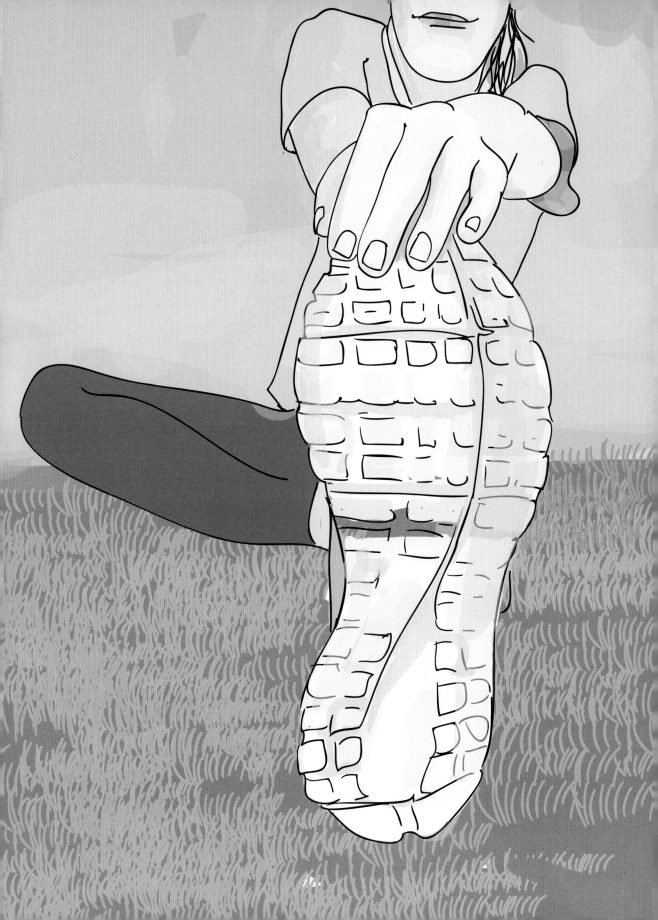

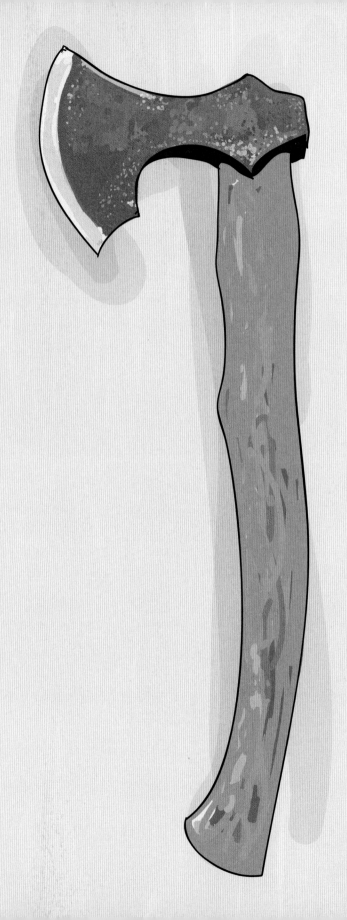

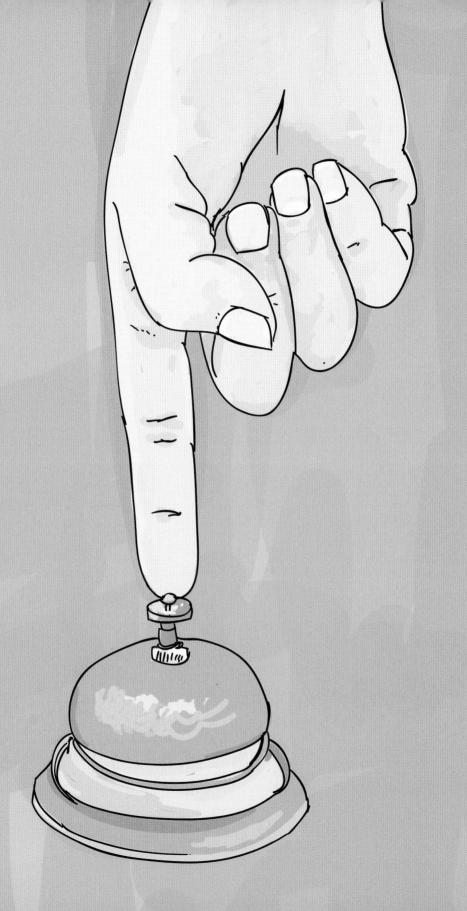

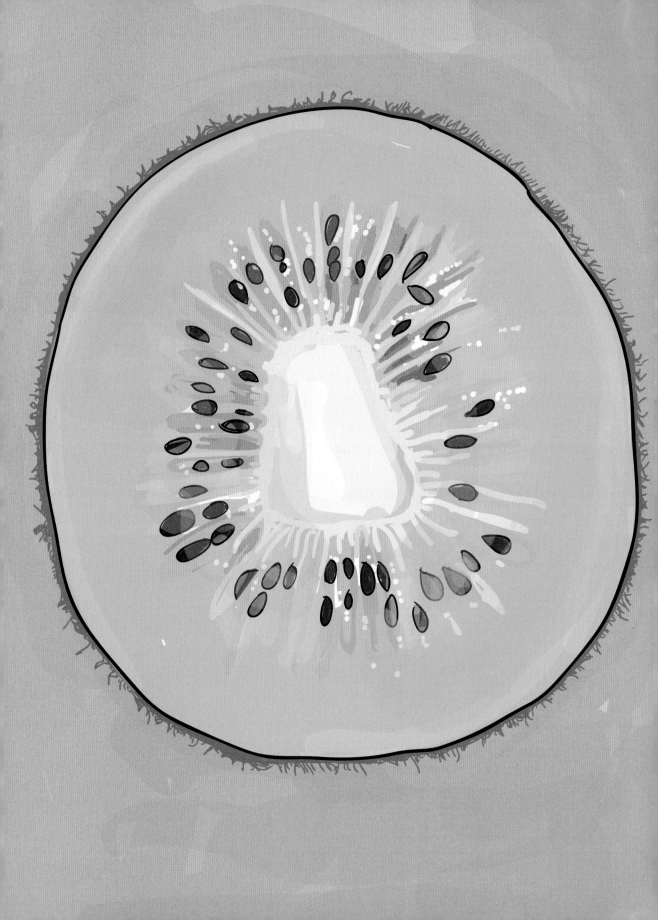

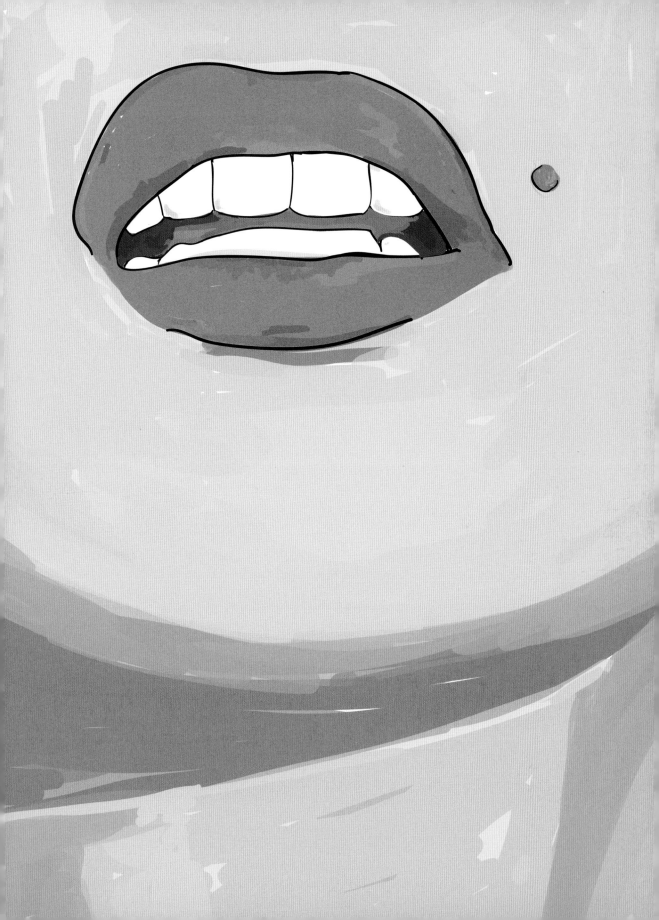

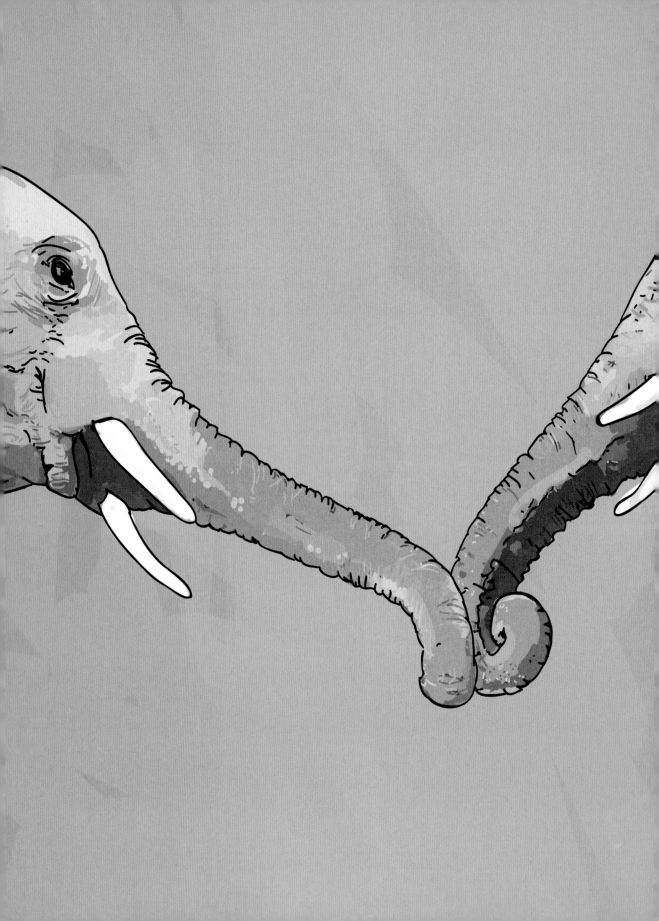

One *boxer* is able to bark
and the other has a strong arm.

The *crane* on the left can lift heavy
things up in the air.
The one on the right will fly away.

You can dance at a *ball* or
you can play with one.

You put your *palm* in the air to wave
and say goodbye.
A *palm* tree's leaves can wave in the wind.

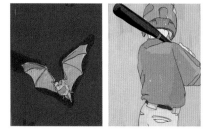

In the darkness the *bat* is coming.
In the daytime you can swing a *bat*.

Inside a *bank* you can deposit
your money and outside you can reach a
bank when swimming in a sea.

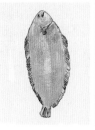

The *sole* is a fish that lives on the
sea bottom. You can find a *sole* on the
bottom of your shoe.

It's exciting to ride in a *chopper*
or to use one to cut wood.

You can use *sink* water to
wash the dishes but too much water
can *sink* a ship.

Sisters always belong together!

Like the insect,
the girl in the picture will *fly* away.

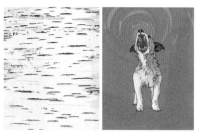

Tree *bark* can be prickly to the touch.
A dog's *bark* can
sound prickly in your ears!

Some girls dream of an impressive *ring*. When you arrive at your friend's door you can *ring* a bell.

The army will roll out a *tank* only in case of an emergency, maybe when the shark has jumped out of its *tank*!

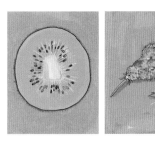

A *kiwi* is a green fruit and it's also a cute bird that cannot fly.

When a *wave* is high you can surf on it. When you see the Queen she will *wave* at you.

Odd couples and the *words* that bring them together

An *Iris* is the colourful part of the eye or a special, colourful flower.

A *cardinal* can be a holy man or a beautiful bird. You will be blessed if you see either one.

The male *buck* uses its big horns to fight. You can use the other *buck* to spend one dollar.

A *tip* is good for the waiter but watch out for the *tip* of an iceberg!

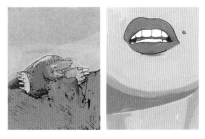

Marilyn Monroe's *mole* was the most beautiful on earth. A burrowing *mole* isn't so pretty.

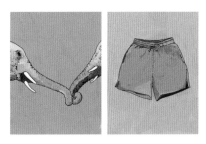

Feed the *trunks* with peanuts or just go swimming with them!

© 2017, Prestel Verlag, Munich · London · New York
A member of Verlagsgruppe Random House GmbH
Neumarkter Strasse 28 · 81673 Munich

© for the illustrations: 2017, Mirja Winkelmann, www.mirjawinkelmann.com

Prestel Publishing Ltd.
14-17 Wells Street
London W1T 3PD

Prestel Publishing
900 Broadway, Suite 603
New York, NY 10003

In respect to links in the book, the Publisher expressly notes that no illegal content was
discernible on the linked sites at the time the links were created. The Publisher has no
influence at all over the current and future design, content or authorship of the linked sites.
For this reason the Publisher expressly disassociates itself from all content on linked
sites that has been altered since the link was created and assumes no liability for such content.

Library of Congress Control Number: 2016960247
A CIP catalogue record for this book is available from the British Library.

Editorial direction: Doris Kutschbach
Design and layout: Mirja Winkelmann
Production management: Corinna Pickart
Separations: Reproline Mediateam, Munich
Printing and binding: DZS Grafik, d.o.o., Ljubljana
Paper: Profimatt

Verlagsgruppe Random House FSC® N001967
Printed in Slovenia

ISBN 978-3-7913-7291-4
www.prestel.com